Picnics

Picnics

David Herbert photography by David Loftus

Lunch on the Road

1 small chicken
2 teaspoons olive oil for roasting
6 tablespoons mayonnaise
2 tablespoons chopped fresh chives
12 slices white bread
50g (2oz) butter, softened
salt and freshly ground black pepper

1 tablespoon vegetable oil
8 rashers streaky bacon, cut into 2cm (¾in) strips
½ small brown onion, thinly sliced
500g (1lb) ready-made puff pastry
1 egg, lightly beaten, to glaze
1 medium potato, peeled and thinly sliced
175g (6oz) matured cheddar cheese, coarsely grated
salt and freshly ground black pepper

Chicken and chive sandwiches
Serves 4–6
Preparation time: 1½ hours, plus cooling

In the kitchen – To roast the chicken, place it in a roasting tin in an oven preheated to 200°C (400°F), gas mark 6. Rub the skin with the olive oil. Cook the chicken for 20 minutes per 500g (1lb), plus an extra 20 minutes. Alternatively, place it whole in a large saucepan, cover it with water, bring to the boil and simmer gently for 1 hour. Remove the cooked chicken from the oven or saucepan and set it aside to cool.

Pull the meat from the chicken and cut or shred the flesh into small pieces. Place the meat in a bowl and add enough mayonnaise to bind the mix. Mix in the chives and season well with salt and freshly ground black pepper.

Spread the bread lightly with the softened butter. Divide the chicken mixture between 6 slices of bread and top with the remaining 6 slices. Remove the crusts if desired, wrap in plastic wrap or greaseproof paper and store in an airtight container in the refrigerator until ready to take to the picnic.
At the picnic – Unwrap the sandwiches and cut each one into three fingers.

Bacon, cheese and potato pie
Serves 8
Preparation time: 1 hour 10 minutes

In the kitchen – Heat the oil in a large frying pan and cook the bacon, stirring occasionally, for 2 minutes. Add the onion and cook for 4–5 minutes or until softened, but not coloured. Allow to cool.

Preheat the oven to 200°C (400°F), gas mark 6.

Divide the pastry into 2 portions. Roll out the first to form a 25cm (10in) diameter circle. Lay the pastry circle on a lightly greased baking tray and brush with beaten egg. Spread the bacon and onion mixture evenly over the pastry, leaving a 2cm (¾in) border all the way around. Top with the potato slices and then the grated cheese, seasoning each layer.

Roll the second piece of pastry to form a 28cm (11in) diameter circle. Place it over the filling and press the edges together to join. Trim, knock up the edges and cut a cross in the middle of the pie. Bake for 10 minutes, then reduce the heat to 180°C (350°F), gas mark 4 and cook for a further 30 minutes, or until golden and risen.

Allow the pie to cool slightly on the baking sheet before transferring it to a wire rack to cool. Slide the pie onto a plate and cover with plastic wrap to transport it to the picnic.
At the picnic – Cut the pie into 8 wedges and serve.

3 tablespoons grated fresh ginger
250g (8oz) sugar
1 teaspoon grated lemon zest
375ml (13fl oz) water
juice of 2 lemons
lemon slices
mint sprigs
chilled water, to dilute

125g (4oz) sugar
375ml (13fl oz) water
6 oranges
1 lemon
chilled water, to dilute

Ginger drink
Makes about 450ml (¾ pint) syrup
Preparation time: 20 minutes

In the kitchen – Place the ginger, sugar, zest and water in a small saucepan. Bring the mixture to the boil, stirring constantly to dissolve the sugar. Simmer for 5 minutes. Allow to cool. Strain through a fine sieve into a jug, add the lemon juice and then pour the mixture into a bottle. Seal, label and store in the refrigerator for up to 5 days. This makes a delicious base which is then diluted with still or sparkling mineral water or soda water as needed.

At the picnic – Dilute 1 part ginger syrup to 5 parts water. Garnish with lemon slices and mint.

Orangeade
Makes about 1 litre (1¾pints) syrup
Preparation time: 20 minutes

In the kitchen – Place the sugar and water in a saucepan. With a sharp knife, vegetable peeler or zester remove the zest from 2 of the oranges, being careful to leave behind any white pith. Cut the zest into thin strips and add it to the saucepan. Bring the mixture to the boil, stirring constantly to dissolve the sugar. Simmer for 5 minutes.

Squeeze the juice of all six oranges and the lemon and pour into the saucepan. Allow to cool. Strain through a fine sieve into a jug and then pour the mixture into a bottle. Seal, label and store in the refrigerator for up to 5 days. This makes a delicious base which is then diluted with still or sparkling mineral water or soda water as needed.

At the picnic – Dilute 1 part orange syrup to 5 parts water.

Travelling by car means there's one important thing you don't have to worry about – weight. Pack your picnic in a proper hamper with china plates and cups and real cutlery. You can even go for the full Fifties' experience and put a folding table and chair set in the boot. Turning your car into a travelling deli beats motorway fare hands down. Refreshing ginger syrup and real orangeade will keep drivers alert, while substantial beef rolls, chicken sandwiches and a bacon, cheese and potato pie will boost everyone's energy levels. Pull off the road and find a quiet layby. No need to worry about the weather – none of these recipes are so awkward to eat that you risk spoiling the upholstery if you do end up picnicking in the car.

500g (1lb) piece of beef fillet or topside
2 garlic cloves, sliced
4 crusty white bread rolls or a large French stick
  cut into 4
25g (1oz) butter, softened
3 tablespoons Dijon mustard
large handful rocket (arugula) leaves
salt and freshly ground black pepper

1 large round crusty Italian-style bread loaf
extra-virgin olive oil
12 slices salami
200g (7oz) mozzarella, sliced
12 slices mortadella
50g (2oz) rocket (arugula) leaves, trimmed
3 vine-ripened tomatoes, sliced
20 basil leaves
salt and freshly ground black pepper

Roast beef and mustard rolls

Serves 4
Preparation time: 50 minutes

In the kitchen – Preheat the oven to 220°C (425°F), gas
mark 7. Cut narrow slits into the beef and insert 3 or 4 slices
of garlic. Roast the beef in the oven for 25 minutes (for
medium rare), or until cooked to your liking. Set aside to
cool, then cut the beef into thin slices.

Split the bread rolls in half, butter them lightly and spread
them with mustard. Divide the beef slices between the rolls.
Spoon over any juices from the pan. Season the beef with salt
and freshly ground black pepper. Top with some rocket.

Wrap the rolls in greaseproof paper and secure the parcels
with string.

Pan bagna

Serves 4
Preparation time: 15 minutes, plus chilling time

In the kitchen – Make the pan bagna the night before you
plan to eat it. Slice off the top of the loaf and reserve.
Remove all the soft bread filling from the loaf, leaving the
crust to form a case. Brush the inside of the bread with a
little extra-virgin olive oil.

Layer the loaf with the salami, mozzarella, mortadella,
rocket leaves, tomato slices and basil, pressing well on each
layer and seasoning with salt and freshly ground black pepper
as you go. When the bread case is full, drizzle with a little
extra olive oil and replace the bread lid. Press the lid firmly in
place and wrap the loaf tightly in a couple of layers of plastic
wrap. Place in the refrigerator and place a weight or heavy
breadboard on top and chill overnight. Transport to the
picnic wrapped in the plastic wrap.

At the picnic – To serve, unwrap and cut the loaf into
quarters with a sharp knife.

Variations

Choose and vary the filling ingredients to suit your taste.
Try using thinly sliced grilled aubergine, roasted red peppers
or marinated artichokes.

250g (8oz) unsalted butter, softened
250g (8oz) caster (superfine) sugar
250g (8oz) self-raising (self-rising) flour
2 teaspoons baking powder
pinch salt
4 eggs, lightly beaten
75ml (3fl oz) milk
1 tablespoon grated lemon zest

Icing:
125g (4oz) icing sugar, sifted
25g (1oz) butter, softened
2–3 tablespoons lemon juice

Base:
2 eggs
125g (4oz) caster (superfine) sugar
120ml (4fl oz) single cream
1 tablespoon grated orange zest
150g (5oz) self-raising (self-rising) flour

Topping:
100g (3½oz) butter, cubed
100g (3½oz) caster (superfine) sugar
60ml (2fl oz) single cream
1 heaped tablespoon plain (all-purpose) flour
2 teaspoons grated orange zest
100g (3½oz) flaked almonds

Iced lemon cake

Serves 6
Preparation time: 55–60 minutes

In the kitchen – Preheat the oven to 180°C (350°F),
gas mark 4.

Grease a 20 x 30cm (8 x 12in) shallow cake tin and line
the base with baking paper.

Place all the cake ingredients in a large mixing bowl
and, using an electric beater, beat them at a low speed for
2 minutes. Increase the speed to medium and beat for
another 2 minutes, or until the mixture is smooth and drops
easily off a spoon. Spoon the mixture into the prepared tin
and smooth the surface.

Bake the cake for 45–50 minutes, or until golden and firm
to the touch – a skewer inserted into the centre of the cake
should come out clean. Allow the cake to cool in the tin.

Make the icing by mixing together the icing sugar, butter
and lemon juice with a wooden spoon, until smooth. Add a
little extra lemon juice or hot water if needed to achieve a
spreadable consistency. Spread the icing over the cake.
At the picnic – Transport to your picnic spot in the cake tin
and cut it into slices when ready to serve.

Orange and almond tray bake

Makes 24 slices
Preparation time: 40–45 minutes

In the kitchen – Preheat the oven to 180°C (350°F),
gas mark 4.

Grease a 20 x 30cm (8 x 12in) shallow cake tin and line
the base with baking paper.

To make the cake base, lightly beat the eggs, sugar, cream
and orange zest together until combined. Gradually beat in
the flour until smooth. Spoon the mixture into the prepared
tin and bake for 15–20 minutes, or until golden.

Meanwhile, make the topping by melting the butter in a
small saucepan over a low heat. Stir in the sugar, cream and
flour and continue to cook, stirring well until the mixture
boils and becomes slightly thickened. Remove from the heat
and stir in the orange zest and flaked almonds. Spread the
topping over the base and return to the oven for a further
15 minutes, or until the cake is golden brown. Allow the
cake to cool in the tin.
At the picnic – Transport to your picnic spot in the cake tin
and cut it into slices when ready to serve.

Picnic on a Boat

1.5kg (3lb) ripe tomatoes
500ml (16fl oz) tomato juice
1 small cucumber, peeled and roughly chopped
1 red pepper (bell pepper), deseeded and chopped
2 cloves garlic, chopped
1 small red (Spanish) onion, chopped
2 thick slices good white bread
250ml (8fl oz) water
3 tablespoons sherry vinegar or red wine vinegar
1 tablespoon chopped fresh basil
Tabasco sauce
salt and freshly ground black pepper
extra-virgin olive oil, to drizzle

250g (8oz) ripe cherry tomatoes
4 large sweet ripe tomatoes
3 tablespoons extra-virgin olive oil
1½ tablespoons balsamic vinegar
1 clove garlic, crushed and finely chopped
1 tablespoon shredded fresh mint leaves
salt and freshly ground black pepper

Gazpacho
Serves 6
Preparation time: 20 minutes, plus chilling time

In the kitchen – Use a sharp knife to cut a cross in the base of each tomato. Place in a heatproof bowl and cover with boiling water. Leave for 45 seconds, then transfer to cold water and peel the skin away, beginning at the cross. Roughly chop the tomatoes, reserving any liquid and place the tomatoes, reserved liquid, tomato juice, cucumber, red pepper, garlic and onion in a large mixing bowl. Remove the crusts from the bread. Chop the bread and add it to the bowl. Stir in the water.

Transfer the mixture to a food processor or blender and pulse until the mixture is roughly combined. (This may need to be done in batches.) The mixture should still be slightly chunky. Add a little extra water if the soup needs thinning.

Chill for at least 2 hours, or preferably overnight, to allow the flavours to develop. Stir in the vinegar, basil and a few drops of Tabasco sauce. Season to taste with salt and freshly ground black pepper.

Transfer the soup to a large, wide-mouthed thermos and add a couple of ice cubes, if available.

At the picnic – Pour into small mugs and drizzle with a little extra-virgin olive oil.

Tomato and mint salad
Serves 4
Preparation time: 10 minutes

You can use a variety of tomatoes in this salad. Try to find at least two different varieties. I recommend using some cherry or small sweet tomatoes along with a large fleshier variety. You can make this up to 2 hours before your picnic.

In the kitchen – Halve the cherry tomatoes and place them in a bowl. Cut the large tomatoes into quarters or small wedges and add them to the bowl of cherry tomatoes. Pour the oil and balsamic vinegar over the tomatoes, then stir in the garlic and mint. Season the tomatoes well with salt and freshly ground black pepper. Transfer to a lidded container to transport to the picnic.

At the picnic – Stir, taste and season with a little extra salt and pepper if needed. Serve in a bowl.

1kg (2lb) waxy salad potatoes, scrubbed
2–3 tablespoons chopped chives or mint
4 finely sliced spring onions (scallions)
½ small red (Spanish) onion, finely sliced
2 tablespoons olive oil
1 tablespoon lemon juice
½ teaspoon Dijon mustard
100ml (3½fl oz) good quality mayonnaise
salt and freshly ground black pepper

500g (1lb) fresh ricotta
1 clove of garlic, peeled and finely chopped
2 tablespoons chopped chives
1 teaspoon grated lemon zest
2 egg whites
extra-virgin olive oil, to drizzle
salt and freshly ground black pepper
crusty bread, to serve

Potato salad

Serves 4
Preparation time: 20 minutes

In the kitchen – Cook the potatoes in a large saucepan of gently boiling salted water for 12–15 minutes, or until just tender. Drain and allow to cool slightly.

While the potatoes are still warm, cut them into 2cm (¾in) pieces and place them in a large bowl with the herbs, spring onions and red onion. Season well with salt and freshly ground black pepper.

Drizzle the potatoes with olive oil and lemon juice and mix gently to coat. Allow to cool. Combine the Dijon mustard and mayonnaise and transport the mixture to the picnic in a sealed container.

At the picnic – Gently fold the mustard mayonnaise through the potato salad, taking care not to break up the potatoes. Taste and season if necessary.

Baked ricotta

Serves 6
Preparation time: 1 hour–1 hour 10 minutes

In the kitchen – Preheat the oven to 180°C (350°F), gas mark 4. Grease a 750ml (1¼pint) deep-sided, ovenproof dish with butter or oil. Place the ricotta in a bowl and stir in the garlic, chives and lemon zest. Season to taste with salt and freshly ground black pepper.

Beat the egg whites until they begin to form soft peaks. Gently fold a little of the egg whites through the ricotta to slacken the mixture, and then carefully fold in the remaining whites. Spoon the mixture into the dish, smooth the top and drizzle with extra-virgin olive oil.

Bake for 45–55 minutes, or until the mixture is set, risen and golden. Allow it to cool in the ovenproof dish and cover with plastic wrap. Use the same dish to transport the baked ricotta to the picnic.

At the picnic – Spread the baked ricotta onto crusty bread or cut it into pieces and serve with Tomato and Mint Salad (page 18).

500g (1lb) black or green olives
3 garlic cloves, crushed
1 large red chilli, seeded and finely chopped
2 teaspoons chopped lemon zest
2 teaspoons chopped rosemary
3 sprigs thyme
2 bay leaves
olive oil

8 ripe figs
8 thin slices prosciutto
extra-virgin olive oil
balsamic vinegar
freshly ground black pepper

Marinated olives

Serves 6
Preparation time: 5 minutes, plus marinating

In the kitchen – Combine the olives, garlic, chilli, lemon
zest, rosemary, thyme and bay leaves in a mixing bowl, then
spoon into a large glass jar. Add enough olive oil to cover the
olives. Seal the jar and tap gently to dislodge any air bubbles.
   Store in the refrigerator to marinate for at least 3 days
before eating.

Variations

You can use many other flavour combinations for this
versatile dish. Chopped orange zest, basil leaves or anchovies
are just a few other ingredients that work well. Vary the
recipe above with one or more of these.
   The olives may be stored in a refrigerator, covered with oil,
for up to 3 weeks.

Figs and prosciutto

Serves 4
Preparation time: 5 minutes

In the kitchen – Using a small sharp knife, carefully peel the
figs. Wrap each fig with a slice of prosciutto and place them
in an airtight container. Pour some oil and vinegar into
separate screw-top containers to take to the picnic.
At the picnic – Drizzle each wrapped fig with a little extra-
virgin olive oil and a few drops of balsamic vinegar. Season
them with a little freshly ground black pepper.

6 large eggs
100g (3½oz) baby spinach leaves, roughly chopped
pinch grated nutmeg
150g (5oz) grated Parmesan cheese
1 tablespoon olive oil
200g (7oz) feta cheese, cut into ½ cm cubes
salt and freshly ground black pepper

1kg (2lb) salmon fillets
250g (8oz) asparagus
150g (5oz) French green beans
50g (2oz) rocket (arugula)
125ml (4fl oz) virgin olive oil
1 clove garlic, crushed
1 tablespoon chopped chives
3 tablespoons lemon juice
2 tablespoons balsamic vinegar
salt and freshly ground black pepper

Spinach and feta frittata
Serves 4
Preparation time: 25 minutes

A frittata is perfect picnic fare. It is also good cut into small pieces and served as part of an antipasto plate or as a snack.

In the kitchen – Break the eggs into a mixing bowl and beat lightly with a fork. Stir through the spinach, nutmeg and 125g (4oz) of the Parmesan cheese. Season to taste with salt and freshly ground black pepper.

Heat the olive oil in a 23cm (9in) non-stick frying pan over a medium heat. Swirl the pan to coat with oil. Pour in the egg mixture, stirring once. Turn the heat to low. Sprinkle the feta over the frittata and cook for 12–15 minutes until the bottom is firm and the top just a little runny. Sprinkle with the remaining grated Parmesan.

Place the frying pan under a preheated grill, just long enough to set the top. A good frittata should be firm and moist, never stiff and dry. Remove and set aside to cool.

Place a large flat plate over the top of the pan and invert the frittata onto it. Wrap the plate and frittata in plastic wrap and keep chilled.

At the picnic – Serve the frittata sliced into wedges.

Variations
Try incorporating cooked courgettes (zucchini), sautéed mushrooms, cooked asparagus, prosciutto, marinated artichokes, goat's cheese or cooked potato slices.

Salmon, asparagus and rocket salad
Serves 4
Preparation time: 20 minutes

In the kitchen – Preheat the oven to 180°C (350°F), gas mark 4. Season the salmon fillets with salt and pepper, place them in a baking tray and roast them (skin-side down) in the oven for 10 minutes, or until they are cooked through. Remove from oven and set aside to cool.

Meanwhile, trim any woody ends from the asparagus and cook them in a large saucepan of boiling salted water until tender, but still slightly crunchy. Using tongs, remove the asparagus from the pan, drain on kitchen paper and set aside to cool. Bring the water back to the boil and cook the beans for 3 minutes, or until tender.

To transport, remove the skin from the salmon and wrap the salmon fillets in foil. Dry the vegetables with kitchen paper and wrap them in foil. Pack the rocket in a sturdy lidded container to protect it from being crushed. Put the oil, garlic, chives, lemon juice and balsamic vinegar into a screw top jar.

At the picnic – To assemble the salad, place the rocket and asparagus and beans on a large platter. Flake the fish into bite-size pieces and scatter them over the rocket and vegetables. Shake the dressing and lightly dress the salad. Season with salt and freshly ground black pepper.

100ml (3½fl oz) olive oil
1 garlic clove, crushed
1 sprig rosemary, chopped
½ teaspoon crushed dried chilli flakes
4 small pitta breads
salt and freshly ground black pepper

2 large sweet potatoes
vegetable oil
salt

Pitta bread crisps
Serves 4
Preparation time: 15 minutes

In the kitchen – Preheat oven to 200°C (400°F), gas mark 6.

Combine the oil, garlic, rosemary and chilli flakes in a small bowl. Using a sharp knife, split each piece of bread in half, giving you 8 flat discs. Brush both sides of each bread disc with the flavoured oil and season with a little salt and freshly ground black pepper.

Place the bread in a single layer on 2 baking sheets and bake, turning once, for 5–10 minutes, or until golden. Break into pieces to serve. Store in an airtight container.

At the picnic – Serve with drinks.

Sweet potato crisps
Serves 4
Preparation time: 20 minutes

In the kitchen – Peel the sweet potatoes and slice very thinly with a vegetable peeler, mandolin or sharp knife. Place enough oil in a deep frying or sauté pan to reach a depth of 2½cm (1in). Heat the oil to 180°C (350°F) and deep-fry the slices, a few at a time for 3–4 minutes, turning occasionally. When they are crisp and golden, remove them with a slotted spoon and drain on kitchen paper. Store the crisps in an airtight container.

At the picnic – Sprinkle well with salt and serve with drinks.

50g (2oz) unsalted butter, cubed
125ml (4fl oz) golden syrup
125g (4oz) plain (all-purpose) flour
40g (1¾ oz) self-raising (self-rising) flour
1 teaspoon bicarbonate of soda (sodium bicarbonate)
4 heaped tablespoons cocoa
125g (4oz) caster (superfine) sugar
pinch of salt
125ml (4fl oz) milk
1 egg, beaten
icing sugar

175g (6oz) unsalted butter
50g (2oz) plain (all-purpose) flour
175g (6oz) icing sugar, plus extra to serve
100g (3½oz) ground almonds
2 teaspoons finely grated lemon zest
5 egg whites
16 raspberries

Simple sticky chocolate cake

Serves 8
Preparation time: 1 hour 10 minutes

In the kitchen – Preheat the oven to 170°C (325°F), gas mark 3. Choose a loaf tin with a base that measures 23 x 12cm (9 x 5 in). Grease and line the base with baking paper.

Place the butter and golden syrup in a small saucepan over a low heat and melt, stirring occasionally. Remove the pan from the heat.

Sift both types of flour, the bicarbonate of soda, cocoa, sugar and salt into a mixing bowl. Add the milk and beaten egg and mix until smooth. Gradually add the melted butter mixture, stirring until well incorporated.

Pour the batter into the prepared loaf tin and bake for 50–55 minutes, or until the cake has risen and is firm to the touch. A skewer inserted into the middle of the cake should come out clean.

Allow the cake to cool in the tin. Dust with a little icing sugar and transport to the picnic in the tin.

At the picnic – Turn the cake out of the tin and slice.

Little almond and raspberry cakes

Makes 8
Preparation time: 35 minutes

In the kitchen – Preheat the oven to 200°C (400°F), gas mark 6. Lightly grease 8 small brioche tins (measuring 8cm (3½in) at widest part across the top with 75ml/ 3fl oz capacity) or a 12 cup mini muffin tin or cupcake tin.

Melt the butter in a small saucepan over a low heat, and cook for 30–45 seconds or until golden, being careful not to burn the butter.

Sift the flour and icing sugar into a mixing bowl. Stir in the ground almonds and lemon zest.

Lightly beat the egg whites with a fork until they are frothy and pour them into the bowl along with the dry ingredients. Add the warm butter and mix with a wooden spoon until smooth.

Spoon the mixture into the prepared brioche tins, filling each three-quarters full and topping each with 2 raspberries.

Bake the cakes for 5 minutes, then reduce the heat to 180°C (350°F), gas mark 4 and cook for a further 10–15 minutes, or until they are golden and risen. Allow them to cool in the tins. Dust each cake with a little icing sugar and transport them to the picnic in the tins.

At the picnic – Turn the cakes out of the tins and serve them plain or with fresh berries.

Teatime in the Park

1 mint tea bag
2 Ceylon tea bags
100g (3½oz) caster (superfine) sugar
750ml (1¼ pints) boiling water
juice of 2 limes
juice of 1 lemon
lime slices
fresh mint leaves

250g (8oz) caster (superfine) sugar
350ml (12fl oz) water
8 fresh mint leaves
6 lemons
chilled water, to dilute

Iced tea with lime and mint
Makes approximately 900ml (1½ pints) tea
Preparation time: 10 minutes, plus chilling

In the kitchen – Place the tea bags and sugar in a large teapot or heatproof jug and pour in the boiling water. Stir well to dissolve the sugar and leave the tea to infuse for 8–10 minutes. Remove the tea bags and leave the tea to cool. Stir in the lime juice and lemon juice and chill or freeze until ready to transport.
At the picnic – Transport the chilled tea to the picnic spot in a large, sealed, unbreakable jug. Serve in tall glasses garnished with lime slices and mint leaves.

Lemonade with mint
Makes approximately 1 litre (1¾ pints) syrup
Preparation time: 10 minutes, plus chilling

In the kitchen – Place the sugar, water and mint leaves in a saucepan. Using a sharp knife, vegetable peeler or zester remove the zest of one lemon, being careful to leave behind any white pith. Cut the zest into thin strips and add it to the saucepan. Bring the mixture to the boil, stirring constantly to dissolve the sugar. Simmer for 5 minutes.
Squeeze the juice of all six lemons and add to the saucepan. Allow to cool. Strain the mixture through a fine sieve into a jug and then pour it into a bottle. Seal, label and store in the refrigerator for up to 5 days.
This makes a delicious base which is then diluted with still or sparkling mineral water or soda water as needed.
At the picnic – Dilute 1 part lemon syrup to 5 parts water.

Let's face it what we all really want at teatime – grown-ups and children alike – is cake, and lots of it. Keep sandwiches low key – but delicious – and concentrate on a selection of sweet things, from rich fruit cake, moist banana bread to wickedly chocolatey muffins. The recipes here are quite sophisticated, making this more of an adults' teatime picnic but children may be tempted to join in too for the cupcakes and the chocolate salami. Serve refreshing citrus-spiked iced tea to the grown ups and homemade lemonade to any children. Keep picnic equipment simple: plastic beakers, paper napkins and a picnic rug should do the trick. Wrap as much of the food as you can in disposable wrappers. Fewer picnic containers, and no plates and cutlery means virtually no washing up. Here's how you can turn an ordinary day into something special by taking tea to the park.

24 spears asparagus
125g (4oz) mild goat's cheese
12 slices brown or white bread
25g (1oz) butter, softened

200g (7oz) caster (superfine) sugar
300ml (½ pint) water
300g (10oz) whole almonds
50g (2oz) glacé fruit, chopped
100g (3½oz) cocoa, sifted
200g (7oz) icing sugar, sifted

Asparagus and goat's cheese sandwiches
Serves 6
Preparation time: 10 minutes

In the kitchen – Cook the asparagus, either by steaming for 5–6 minutes or boiling in a large pan of salted water for 4–6 minutes, or until just tender – be careful not to overcook it. Drain the spears, rinse them in cold water and dry well with kitchen paper.

Spread 6 slices of bread thickly with the goat's cheese or cut the cheese into thin slices and lay on the bread. Top each slice with 4 asparagus spears. Spread the remaining 6 slices of bread lightly with the softened butter and use them to top each sandwich.

Remove the crusts from the sandwiches if you want to, then wrap in plastic wrap or in a lightly damp cloth and store in an airtight container in the refrigerator until needed.

At the picnic – Unwrap the sandwiches and cut each one into 2 fingers before serving.

Chocolate salami
Serves 10–12
Preparation time: 10 minutes plus chilling

In the kitchen – Combine the sugar and water in a large saucepan over a medium heat, stirring to dissolve the sugar. Bring to the boil and boil steadily for 3 minutes. Remove from the heat and stir in the almonds, crystallized fruit and cocoa. Return to the heat and cook, stirring continuously, for 2 minutes – the mixture should turn into a thick mass.

Sprinkle half the icing sugar on the worktop. Turn out the chocolate mixture onto the icing sugar and roll into a log approximately 5cm (2in) in diameter. Leave to cool, then roll the log in extra icing sugar to give a white coating.

Wrap in foil and chill for 6 hours.

At the picnic – Unwrap the chocolate salami and slice it into 5mm (¼in) rounds.

225g (7½oz) self-raising (self-rising) flour
125g (4oz) unsalted butter, softened
125g (4oz) caster (superfine) sugar
1 teaspoon grated orange zest
1 egg, lightly beaten
2 eggs yolks, lightly beaten
100ml (3½fl oz) orange juice

Topping:
125g (4oz) granulated sugar
75ml (3fl oz) orange juice

Orange drizzle cupcakes
Makes 12
Preparation time: 40 minutes

In the kitchen – Preheat the oven to 180°C (350°F), gas mark 4. Line a 12 hole cupcake tin with paper cases.

Sift the flour into a large mixing bowl. Add the butter, sugar, orange zest, eggs and juice. Beat the mixture using an electric beater set to medium speed, for 3 minutes, or until the ingredients are fully combined.

Spoon the mixture evenly into the paper cases. Bake for 15–20 minutes, or until they are golden and firm to the touch. A skewer inserted in the centre of a cupcake should come out clean. Remove the cupcakes from the tin while still hot and place them on a wire rack.

To make the topping, roughly mix together the granulated sugar and orange juice. Don't dissolve the sugar – it should form a sugary slurry. Quickly spoon the topping evenly over the top of the hot cakes. The juice will sink into the cakes and the sugar will form a crunchy topping when cool.

To transport the cupcakes to the picnic, pack them into an airtight container, placing sheets of baking paper between any layers.

At the picnic – Serve the cupcakes in their paper cases.

2 egg whites
125g (4oz) ground hazelnuts
175g (6oz) caster (superfine) sugar
2 tablespoons cornflour (corn starch)
grated zest of 1 orange
1 teaspoon vanilla essence

Hazelnut macaroons
Makes 12
Preparation time: 30 minutes

In the kitchen – Preheat the oven to 160°C (325°F), gas mark 3. Line 2 baking sheets with non-stick baking paper.

Place the egg whites in a large bowl and whisk them for 1–2 minutes, or until frothy – do not let them become stiff.

Stir in the hazelnuts, sugar, cornflour and vanilla essence and mix until combined.

Place tablespoonfuls of the mixture on the prepared baking sheets, allowing 5cm (2in) between each. Bake for 15–20 minutes, or until golden. Remove the macaroons from the oven and allow to cool before storing in an airtight container.

Variations
Make the macaroons with ground almonds if ground hazelnuts are not available.

125g (4oz) butter, softened
100g (3½oz) soft pale brown sugar
50g (2oz) caster (superfine) sugar
2 large eggs
1 teaspoon vanilla essence
175g (6oz) plain (all-purpose) flour
1 teaspoon baking powder
pinch salt
75g (3oz) pecan nuts, chopped
175g (6oz) dark chocolate chips

150g (5oz) dark chocolate, broken into pieces
125g (4oz) butter, cubed
300g (10oz) self-raising (self-rising) flour
½ teaspoon baking powder
pinch salt
4 tablespoons cocoa
250g (8oz) caster (superfine) sugar
175ml (6fl oz) milk
1 teaspoon lemon juice
2 eggs

Chocolate icing:
200g (7oz) dark chocolate, broken into pieces
125g (4oz) soured cream
60g (2½oz) icing sugar

Blondies

Makes 12
Preparation time: 1 hour 10 minutes

In the kitchen – Preheat the oven to 180°C (350°F), gas mark 4. Lightly grease a 23cm (9in) square cake tin and line the base and sides with non-stick baking paper, leaving the paper hanging over the edge on 2 sides. Using an electric beater, beat the butter and sugars together for 3 minutes until fluffy and well mixed. Gradually add the eggs, beating well after each addition. Stir in the vanilla essence.

Sift in the flour, baking powder and salt, and fold them into the mixture. Gently stir in the pecans and chocolate chips. Pour the mixture into the prepared tin and smooth the top with a palette knife. Bake for 30–35 minutes, or until the mixture is golden and the top is just firm. A skewer inserted into the centre should come out clean.

Allow the cake to cool in the tin for 10 minutes, then use the overhanging paper to remove it from the tin. Place it on a wire rack and when cool cut it into squares. Pack the squares in an airtight container, where they will keep fresh for up to 3 days.

Chocolate muffins

Makes 12
Preparation time: 50 minutes

In the kitchen – Grease a 12-hole muffin tin with butter or line with paper muffin cases. Preheat the oven to 180°C (350°F), gas mark 4. Melt the chocolate and butter together in a bowl set over a saucepan of barely simmering water, stirring occasionally until melted and smooth.

Sift the flour, baking powder, salt and cocoa into a mixing bowl. Stir in the sugar and make a well in the centre.

Mix the milk, lemon juice and eggs in a jug and pour them into the flour, followed by the melted chocolate and butter. Mix gently until just combined, but don't over-mix – the batter should still be lumpy.

Divide the mixture between the prepared muffin cases and bake for 20 minutes, or until firm to the touch. Cool in the tin for 10 minutes, then transfer them to a wire rack.

To make the icing, melt the chocolate in a bowl set over a saucepan of barely simmering water, stirring occasionally. Stir in the soured cream and icing sugar and mix until smooth. Remove from heat and spread over the muffins. Alternatively, you could simply dust the muffins with icing sugar.

Store the iced muffins in a single layer in an airtight container to transport to the picnic.

125g (4oz) unsalted butter, softened
250g (8oz) caster (superfine) sugar
2 eggs, lightly beaten
3 very ripe medium bananas
225g (7½oz) plain (all-purpose) flour
1 teaspoon baking powder
1 teaspoon bicarbonate of soda (sodium bicarbonate)
pinch salt
125ml (4fl oz) buttermilk, or milk soured with 2 teaspoons
    lemon juice
150g (5oz) dark chocolate chips
icing sugar, to serve

200g (7oz) whole natural glacé cherries
150g (5oz) mixture glacé fruit (pineapple, apricots,
    citron, mango, etc)
50g (2oz) glacé ginger, roughly chopped
2 teaspoons grated orange zest
3 tablespoons brandy
150g (5oz) whole Brazil nuts
150g (5oz) blanched whole almonds
50g (2oz) butter, melted
1 medium egg, lightly beaten
3 tablespoons soft light brown sugar
75g (3oz) plain (all-purpose) flour
1 teaspoon baking powder
4 tablespoons apricot jam

Banana bread with chocolate chips

Serves 10
Preparation time: 1½ hours

In the kitchen – Preheat the oven to 160°C (325°F), gas
mark 3. Choose a loaf tin with a base that measures 23 x
12cm (9 x 5 in). Grease and line the base with baking paper.

With an electric mixer, beat the butter and sugar for
3–4 minutes, or until pale and fluffy. Gradually add the
beaten eggs, mixing well after each addition.

Mash the bananas with a fork and add them to the
mixture. Stir well to combine.

Sift together the flour, baking powder, bicarbonate of soda
and salt. Gradually add them to the banana mixture,
alternating with the buttermilk and beating well after each
addition. Stir in the chocolate chips.

Spoon the mixture into the prepared tin and bake for
55–60 minutes, or until firm to the touch and a skewer
inserted into the centre comes out clean. Allow to cool in the
tin for 15 minutes before turning out onto a wire rack. Dust
with icing sugar, wrap with plastic wrap and store for up to
3 days. The flavour improves on keeping.

Take the wrapped banana bread to the picnic in its original
loaf tin for easy transport or use an airtight container.

At the picnic – Cut into slices before serving.

American fruit cake

Serves 10–12
Preparation time: 1¾–2 hours plus marinating

In the kitchen – Preheat the oven to 160°C (325°F), gas
mark 3. Choose a loaf tin with a base that measures 23 x
12cm (9 x 5 in). Grease and line the base and sides with
baking paper. Combine the glacé cherries, mixed fruit and
ginger along with the orange zest in a bowl and pour over the
brandy. Set aside to marinate for 1 hour, mixing occasionally.

Stir the nuts into the fruit. Combine the butter, egg and
sugar and stir through the fruit and nut mixture. Sift in
the flour and baking powder and mix until combined.

Spoon the mixture into the loaf tin and smooth the
surface. Bake for 1½ hours, or until golden and firm when
touched. If the top of the cake colours too quickly while
cooking, cover it with piece of foil or baking paper. Leave
the cake to cool in the tin, then remove it from tin, peel off
the paper and brush with warmed apricot jam. Store and
transport the cake in an airtight container.

At the picnic – Slice the fruit cake thinly to serve.

Bike Ride
Picnic

4 fresh eggs
1 tablespoon sea salt flakes
2 teaspoons celery salt
pinch ground chilli
freshly ground black pepper

12 large fresh dates (medjool dates are ideal)
4 tablespoons peanut butter
12 large shelled raw almonds, pecan or walnuts

Hard boiled eggs with spiced salt
Serves 4
Preparation time: 5 minutes plus cooling

In the kitchen – Place the eggs in a saucepan and cover them with cold water. Bring to the boil over a medium heat. Reduce the heat and simmer for 5 minutes.

Using a slotted spoon, remove the eggs from the saucepan and set aside to cool.

To make the spiced salt, combine the sea salt, celery salt, chilli and a grind of black pepper. Store the eggs in the refrigerator in a small lidded container until needed.

At the picnic – Let each picnicker peel their own egg. Pass round the container of spiced salt for dipping the eggs in.

Stuffed dates
Makes 12
Preparation time: 15 minutes

In the kitchen – Remove the stones (pits) from the dates and make a small slit in each with a sharp knife. Fill each date with a teaspoon of peanut butter and stuff with a whole nut. Use a little less peanut butter if the dates are on the small side. Push the dates back into shape and pack them in an airtight container. Store in the refrigerator.

Heading off for a picnic on a bike you'll get a lot further than on foot, especially on a mountain bike. And although you're not carrying a hamper directly, weight is still a consideration, so food that needs minimal packaging – such as hard boiled eggs – is ideal. They will also stand up to rough treatment as your picnic bumps about in a pannier, on your handlebars or in a rucksack. For this picnic the emphasis is on sustenance: robust baguettes, savoury muffins and high-energy chewy bars. Wrapping baguettes in greaseproof paper is a neat trick: it means you'll have something to eat them off and to wipe your fingers on afterwards. Frozen fruit juices that slowly defrost en route to become slushy drinks are the ultimate thirst quenchers. For extra convenience look out for a picnic rug that comes with a carrying strap so that you can sling it over your shoulder as you cycle.

1 baguette or French-style bread stick
olive oil
various fillings, including: salami, pastrami, ham, cheese,
    smoked salmon, sliced tomato, thinly sliced cucumber,
    rocket (arugula) leaves, watercress
salt and freshly ground black pepper

50g (2oz) plain (all-purpose) flour, sifted
½ teaspoon mixed spice
pinch of salt
300g (10oz) quick-cook oats
50g (2oz) desiccated coconut
50g (2oz) sesame seeds
100g (3½oz) sunflower or pumpkin seeds
125g (4oz) dried cranberries
200g (7oz) unsalted butter
125ml (4fl oz) golden syrup
200g (7oz) soft brown sugar
125g (4oz) crunchy peanut butter
1 teaspoon vanilla essence

Wrapped baguettes
Serves 4
Preparation time: 15 minutes

In the kitchen – Make the baguettes on the day of the picnic. Slice the loaf lengthways until almost sliced through. Remove some of the interior of the bread and brush the inside with olive oil. Fill the baguette with your chosen fillings and season with salt and freshly ground black pepper.

Cut the baguette into 4 portions. Wrap each firmly with greaseproof or parchment paper and tie securely with string.

Chewy cranberry bars
Makes 20
Preparation time: 40 minutes

In the kitchen – Preheat the oven to 160°C (325°F), gas mark 3. Grease a 20 x 30cm (8 x 12in) shallow tin and line with baking paper, leaving a little hanging over the two long sides for easy removal.

Sift the flour, mixed spice and salt into a large bowl. Mix in the oats, coconut, sesame seeds, sunflower or pumpkin seeds and dried cranberries.

Put the butter and golden syrup into a saucepan and stir over a low heat until melted. Remove from heat and mix in the sugar, peanut butter and vanilla essence.

Pour the butter mixture into the bowl of dry ingredients and mix with a large metal spoon until combined.

Press the mixture into the prepared tin and bake for 25 minutes or until golden and firm. Allow to cool in the tin, then turn out and cut into 20 squares. Store the bars in an airtight container for up to 7 days. Wrap the bars in greaseproof paper to take to the picnic.

350g (11½oz) self-raising (self-rising) flour
½ teaspoon bicarbonate of soda (sodium bicarbonate)
pinch of salt
2 teaspoons chopped fresh chives
50g (2oz) Parmesan cheese, grated
75g (3oz) feta cheese, cut into 1cm (½in) pieces
150g (5oz) cheddar cheese, grated
300ml (½pint) buttermilk, or milk soured with 2 teaspoons
    lemon juice
2 eggs, lightly beaten
100g (3½oz) butter, melted

Feta, cheddar and chive muffins
Makes 12
Preparation time: 45 minutes

In the kitchen – Preheat the oven to 190°C (375°F), gas
mark 5. Grease a 12 cup muffin tin or line it with paper
muffin cases.

Sift the flour, bicarbonate of soda and salt into a mixing
bowl. Stir in the chives, Parmesan, feta and most of the
cheddar, reserving a little to sprinkle on top. Make a well in
the centre of the dry ingredients.

Whisk together the buttermilk, eggs and melted butter.
Pour the egg mixture into the well and stir until the
ingredients are just combined. Do not over-mix – the batter
should not be smooth.

Divide the mixture evenly between the muffin cups.
Sprinkle with the remaining cheddar cheese and bake for
25–30 minutes, or until the tops are golden and a skewer
inserted into the centre of a muffin comes out clean. Allow
them to cool in the tin for 5 minutes before turning out onto
a wire rack.

Store the muffins in an airtight container.

350g (11½oz) self-raising (self-rising) flour
½ teaspoon bicarbonate of soda (sodium bicarbonate)
125g (4oz) soft brown sugar
pinch of salt
50g (2oz) sultanas
50g (2oz) ground almonds
125ml (4fl oz) buttermilk, or milk soured with 1 teaspoon
    lemon juice
2 eggs, lightly beaten
1 teaspoon vanilla essence
125g (4oz) butter, melted
200g (7oz) marmalade (bitter orange jelly), plus extra
    to decorate
350g (11½oz) carrots (about 3 large ones), finely grated

Carrot and marmalade muffins
Makes 12
Preparation time: 45 minutes

In the kitchen – Preheat the oven to 190°C (375°F), gas
mark 5. Grease a 12 cup muffin tin or line it with paper
muffin cases.

Sift the flour, bicarbonate of soda, sugar and salt into a
mixing bowl. Stir in the sultanas and almonds and make a
well in the centre.

Whisk together the buttermilk, eggs, vanilla essence and
melted butter. Pour the egg mixture into the well in the flour
mixture. Add the marmalade and grated carrots and stir until
the ingredients are just combined. Do not over-mix – the
batter should not be smooth.

Divide the mixture evenly between the muffin cups.
Bake for 20–25 minutes, or until the muffin tops are golden
and a skewer inserted into the centre of a muffin comes out
clean. Allow to cool in the tin for 5 minutes before turning
out onto a wire rack. Brush the tops with a little extra
warmed marmalade.

Store muffins in an airtight container.

4 ripe peaches, peeled and quartered
750ml (1¼ pints) cranberry juice
juice of 1 lime

250g (8oz) strawberries, hulled
1.5kg (3lb) watermelon flesh, roughly chopped
2 teaspoons caster (superfine) sugar
juice of 1 lime

Frozen peach and cranberry juice
Makes 1 litre (1¾ pints)
Preparation time: 15 minutes, plus freezing

In the kitchen – Put the peaches and half the cranberry juice in an electric blender and blend until smooth. Transfer to a large plastic bottle and add the lime juice and remaining cranberry juice.

Seal the bottle and freeze it for at least 4 hours or until frozen solid. Take the frozen bottle on the picnic.

At the picnic – Allow the juice to become slushy, then serve.

Strawberry and watermelon slushy
Makes 1 litre (1¾ pints)
Preparation time: 15 minutes plus freezing

In the kitchen – Purée the strawberries, watermelon and sugar in batches, in an electric blender, until smooth. Transfer to a large plastic bottle and add the lime juice. Seal the bottle and freeze for at least 4 hours or until frozen solid. Take the frozen bottle on the picnic.

At the picnic – Allow the juice to become slushy, then serve.

Beach
Barbecue

3 chicken breasts, skin removed
4 rashers streaky bacon
3 tablespoons olive oil
2 cloves garlic, crushed
juice of ½ lemon
½ teaspoon fresh thyme leaves
salt and freshly ground black pepper
1 lemon, quartered, to serve

Chicken kebabs
Serves 4
Preparation time: 30 minutes plus marinating

In the kitchen – Soak 4 wooden skewers in water for
10 minutes. Cut each chicken breast into 4 equal-sized
pieces. Place 3 pieces of chicken in a row and weave a piece
of bacon between them. Push a skewer through the chicken
and bacon to secure. Separate the chicken pieces a little on
the skewer so that there is a small space between each. Repeat
with the remaining pieces of chicken. Lay the kebabs in a
cermic or glass dish.

Combine the oil, garlic, lemon juice and thyme and brush
the chicken kebabs with the marinade. Leave to marinate in
the refrigerator for up to 4 hours.

At the barbecue – Season each skewer with salt and freshly
ground black pepper and then grill over medium-hot coals,
turning every 2 minutes, for 8–10 minutes or until cooked
through. Serve with lemon quarters.

250ml (8fl oz) natural yogurt
juice of 1 lemon
2 spring onions (scallions), finely chopped
2 cloves of garlic, crushed
3 tablespoons finely chopped fresh mint leaves
750g (1½lb) lamb fillet, cut into large cubes
freshly ground black pepper

Yogurt marinated lamb kebabs
Serves 4–6
Preparation time: 20 minutes plus marinating

In the kitchen – Combine the yogurt, lemon juice, spring
onions, garlic and mint. Place the lamb in a shallow ceramic
or glass dish, season well with black pepper and pour over
the yogurt mixture. Leave to marinate in the refrigerator for
2 hours. Meanwhile soak 4–6 large bamboo skewers in water.
Thread the lamb on the skewers, making sure there is a little
space between each piece of meat.
At the barbecue – Cook the lamb over a medium heat,
turning occasionally, for 8–10 minutes or until cooked to
your liking and lightly charred.

1½kg (3lb) pork spare ribs, cut into pieces
4 tablespoons hoisin sauce
2 tablespoons soy sauce
2 tablespoons tomato ketchup
3 tablespoons dry sherry
2 tablespoons runny honey
juice of 1 lime
2 tablespoons soft pale brown sugar
2 cloves of garlic, crushed
1 tablespoon freshly grated ginger

625g (1¼lb) good quality minced beef
1 small brown onion, finely chopped
1 tablespoon finely chopped fresh flat-leaf parsley
1 tablespoon finely chopped fresh basil
2 tablespoons olive oil
2 teaspoons Dijon-style mustard
salt and freshly ground black pepper
4 burger buns, bread rolls or pitta breads
mustard and tomato ketchup
salad leaves

Spiced spare ribs
Serves 4
Preparation time: 45 minutes plus marinating

In the kitchen – Cook the spare ribs in a large saucepan of boiling salted water for 25 minutes. Drain well. Rinse and dry them with kitchen paper.

Combine the remaining ingredients to make the marinade. Place the ribs in an ovenproof dish and brush with marinade. Leave to marinate for at least 1 hour, ideally for 2 hours. Drain the ribs and wrap them in plastic wrap. Reserve the marinade, pouring it into an airtight container.

At the barbecue – Cook the ribs over a medium heat, turning frequently and basting them with the marinade, for 15–20 minutes, or until cooked and lightly charred.

Beef burgers
Serves 6
Preparation time: 20 minutes

In the kitchen – Mix together the beef, onion, herbs, oil and mustard and season well with salt and plenty of freshly ground black pepper. Using wet hands, shape the mixture into 6 balls, flattening them slightly to form burgers.

At the barbecue – Cook the burgers over a medium heat, turning once, for 3–4 minutes each side, or until cooked to your liking and lightly charred. Warm the buns quickly on the grill. Serve the burgers topped with mustard or ketchup and a few salad leaves.

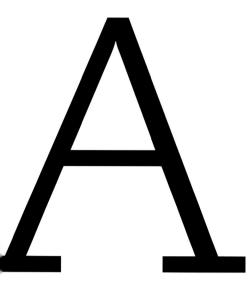

A barbecue on the beach at sunset is hard to beat and good food and a glass of sangria make an evening even more memorable. Kebabs and spare ribs are easy to prepare in advance and are all the better for marinating beforehand – pack any spare marinade in a container to brush on the kebabs as they grill. Some cooks swear by a portable gas barbecue, others prefer a real driftwood fire with an old oven shelf balanced on a couple of rocks for true authenticity but it's probably best to be prepared and take a bag of charcoal at the very least. Don't forget, you'll need a torch or hurricane lamp once the sun goes down or you'll be fumbling for a corkscrew in the dark. And – most important – check the times of the tides in the local paper before you go ahead and invite everyone.

750g (1½lb) small, evenly sized,
   new potatoes, scrubbed
1 sprig rosemary, roughly chopped
1 clove of garlic, crushed
75ml (3fl oz) olive oil
salt and freshly ground black pepper

4 corn cobs, with husks
50g (2oz) butter, softened
salt and freshly ground black pepper

Barbecued new potatoes
Serves 6
Preparation time: 30 minutes

In the kitchen – Soak 6 large bamboo skewers in water.
Cook the potatoes in a large saucepan of boiling salted water
for 12–15 minutes, or until just tender. Drain well and dry
with kitchen paper.

   Stir the rosemary and garlic into the olive oil and store
in a screw-top jar until ready to use.

At the barbecue – Halve the potatoes and thread 4–5 halves
on each skewer. Brush the potatoes with the flavoured oil
and season well with salt and freshly ground black pepper.
Cook the potatoes over a medium heat for 8–10 minutes,
or until lightly charred.

Corn on the cob
Serves 4
Preparation time: 30 minutes

In the kitchen – Place the corn cobs (still in their husks) in a
large pot of boiling salted water. Return to the boil and
simmer for 10 minutes. Remove the cobs from the saucepan
and allow to cool.

   Strip back the husks, remove the silky tassels, and spread
the corn with the softened butter. Season with salt and
freshly ground black pepper. Re-wrap each corn cob in the
husk and tie the husk in place with string.

At the barbecue – Before cooking, soak the corn cobs in a
bowl of water for 2–3 minutes. Grill the corn cobs for
5 minutes, or until heated through and the husk is coloured,
turning them occasionally as they cook.

75g (3oz) butter, cubed
50g (2oz) brown sugar
375g (12oz) block puff pastry, thawed
3 large ripe bananas
50g (2oz) chopped pecans

125g (4oz) butter, chopped
125g (4oz) brown sugar
2 tablespoons water
2 tablespoons rum
2 teaspoons grated lime zest
juice of 1 lime
1 ripe pineapple
mascarpone (optional)

Easy banana tart

Serves 4
Preparation time: 35 minutes

In the kitchen – Preheat the oven to 200°C (400°F), gas mark 6. Put the butter and sugar in a small saucepan and melt over a low heat, stirring occasionally, for 3–4 minutes, or until the butter has melted and the sugar has dissolved. Remove from the heat.

Roll out the pastry on a lightly floured surface to make a 25cm (10in) diameter circle. Lay the pastry circle on a lightly greased baking tray.

Thinly slice the bananas, cutting them diagonally. Spread the banana slices evenly over the pastry in overlapping circles, leaving a 1.5cm (¾in) border all the way around. Sprinkle with pecans. Brush the bananas and nuts with the butter and sugar mixture.

Bake the tart for 15 minutes, or until the pastry has risen and the bananas are golden. Leave the tart to cool then store in an airtight container.

Grilled pineapple

Serves 8
Preparation time: 15 minutes

In the kitchen – Heat the butter, sugar, water, rum and zest in a small saucepan over a low heat, stirring occasionally, until the sugar is dissolved. Remove from the heat and, when cool, store the sauce in a screw-top jar.

Remove the leafy top from the pineapple. Cut off the skin with a sharp knife and slice into 8–10 evenly sized rings. Remove the core from each slice. Store in an airtight container in the refrigerator until needed.

At the barbecue – Brush the pineapple rings with the sauce and grill them for about 5 minutes, or until golden, turning occasionally. Serve immediately with any remaining sauce. Serve with a little mascarpone (if using).

juice of 1 lemon
juice of 1 orange
250ml (8fl oz) peach nectar
500ml (17fl oz) lemonade
60ml (2fl oz) vodka (optional)
750ml (1¼pints) – 1 bottle – fruity white wine
2 fresh ripe peaches, sliced
1 orange, sliced

1 litre (1¾pints) cranberry juice
750ml (1¼pints) –1 bottle – sparkling white wine
60ml (2fl oz) white rum
60ml (2fl oz) Cointreau
2 oranges, sliced
250g (8oz) strawberries, halved
fresh mint leaves

Peach and white wine sangria

Serves 10
Preparation time: 5 minutes plus chilling

In the kitchen – Combine the fruit juices, lemonade and vodka, if using, in a large screw-topped container. Chill in the refrigerator, along with the wine, until needed. Use a coolbag to transport them to the barbecue.

At the barbecue – Pour the chilled juice mixture and wine into a large jug or bowl. Serve the sangria with the sliced fruit and ice, if available.

Cranberry and rum punch

Serves 10
Preparation time: 10 minutes plus chilling

In the kitchen – Chill the cranberry juice and wine in the refrigerator until needed. Use a coolbag to transport them to the barbecue.

At the barbecue – Pour all the liquid ingredients into a large jug or punch bowl, with some ice cubes if available. Add the sliced oranges, strawberries and mint leaves. Mix well and serve in tumblers.

Children's Picnic

1 litre (1¾ pints) cranberry, apple or other
   clear fruit juice
3 x 11g (½oz) sachets powdered gelatine
2 tablespoons caster (superfine) sugar
8 small strawberries
16 raspberries or blackberries

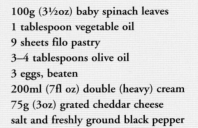

100g (3½oz) baby spinach leaves
1 tablespoon vegetable oil
9 sheets filo pastry
3–4 tablespoons olive oil
3 eggs, beaten
200ml (7fl oz) double (heavy) cream
75g (3oz) grated cheddar cheese
salt and freshly ground black pepper

Jelly cups

Serves 8
Preparation time: 15 minutes, plus chilling

In the kitchen – Place 250ml (8fl oz) of the fruit juice in a
small bowl, sprinkle over the gelatine and leave it to soften
for 5 minutes.

Bring the remaining juice and sugar to the boil in a small
saucepan, stirring to dissolve the sugar. Remove from the
heat and stir through the softened gelatine mixture until the
gelatine has completely dissolved.

Fill 8 small plastic cups three-quarters-full with the jelly
and place them in the refrigerator until the jelly starts to set.
Divide the fruit between the jellies and top with the
remaining liquid jelly. Refrigerate until set, then pack the
cups in a sealable container and keep them chilled until
needed. Don't forget to pack some spoons.

Any fruit or juice combination can be used in this recipe –
except pineapple, which stops the gelatine setting.

Cheese and spinach tarts

Makes 12
Preparation time: 55 minutes

In the kitchen – Preheat the oven to 180°C (350°F),
gas mark 4.

Lightly grease a 12-cup mini muffin tin. Roughly chop the
spinach. Heat the vegetable oil in a large saucepan over a
high heat. Add the spinach, cover and cook for a couple of
minutes until wilted. Remove from the heat and drain well.

Lightly brush 3 sheets of pastry with the olive oil and lay
them on top of each other. Cut four 10cm (4in) circles from
the pastry using a round pastry or cookie cutter. Repeat this
process twice more, giving you a total of 12 pastry circles,
each with 3 layers of pastry. Line the muffin tin with the
pastry circles.

Mix together the eggs and cream and season well with salt
and freshly ground black pepper. Divide the spinach and
grated cheese between the 12 muffin cups and top each with
the cream and egg mixture. Bake for 25–30 minutes or until
the mixture has set and the pastry is golden.

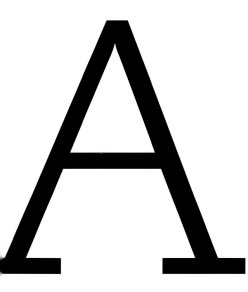children's party is an opportunity to really have some fun. Eating outdoors is exciting for adults, but for kids it's really the ultimate dining experience. (And you don't have to worry about spilt drinks and crumbs squashed into the carpet). For a young child's birthday, organise a teddy bears picnic and ask all the guests to bring along their favourite bear. Make sure you bring along enough food to keep them all happy and include enough variety to cater to a wide range of tastes. Kids love pieces of fresh fruit skewered onto toothpicks and these are an easy and healthy stand-by. A child's party is a great excuse to resurrect a favourite snack of both parents and toddlers – cheese and fresh pineapple toothpicks! Plan a few party games to keep your diners entertained before and after the feast, and maybe pack a bottle of wine or two for deserving adults.

375g (12oz) readymade puff pastry
4 tablespoons tomato ketchup
125g (4oz) cheese, grated
2 tablespoons chopped chives
1 egg, beaten

250g (8oz) ready-made shortcrust pastry, chilled
6 tablespoons good quality berry jam (jelly)

Savoury pastry twists
Makes 4
Preparation time: 45 minutes, plus chilling

In the kitchen – Roll out the pastry to form a 30cm (12in) square. Cut the pastry into 4 equal strips and lay them on a greased baking sheet. Leaving a 1.5cm (¾in) border around each strip of pastry, lightly brush them with the tomato ketchup. Sprinkle the grated cheese evenly over the strips, keeping the cheese inside the border. Top with the chives.

Brush the border of each piece of pastry with a little beaten egg and fold over the pastry so the borders meet, pressing well to seal them firmly. Brush the tops of the pastry parcels with the remaining beaten egg.

Finally, hold one end of the parcel in each hand and twist to form a spiral. Chill in the refrigerator for 30 minutes

Preheat the oven to 200°C (400°F), gas mark 6. Bake the pastry twists for 10–15 minutes, until they are puffed up and golden. Leave to cool then store in an airtight container.

Jam tarts
Makes 12
Preparation time: 25 minutes, plus chilling

In the kitchen – Preheat the oven to 200°C (400°F), gas mark 6. Lightly grease a 12 hole tartlet tin. Remove the pastry from the refrigerator and roll it out between 2 sheets of baking paper. Cut out 12 circles with a 7cm (3in) pastry cutter and line the tartlet tin with the pastry circles. Spoon approximately 2 teaspoons jam into each pastry case, being careful not to over-fill them or the jam will boil over. Chill the tarts for 15 minutes before baking.

Bake the tarts for 10–12 minutes, or until the pastry is golden. Leave to cool in the tin for a few minutes before transferring them to a wire rack to cool completely. Store in an airtight container.

225g (7½oz) self-raising (self-rising) flour, sifted
pinch of salt
125g (4oz) butter, softened
175g (6oz) caster (superfine) sugar
250ml (8fl oz) soured cream
1 teaspoon vanilla essence
finely grated zest of ½ lemon
1 egg
2 egg yolks
125ml (4fl oz) milk

Strawberry icing:
4 ripe strawberries
250g (8oz) icing sugar, sifted

Strawberry cupcakes
Makes 12
Preparation time: 35 minutes

In the kitchen – Preheat the oven to 180°C (350°F), gas mark 4. Line a 12 hole cupcake tin with paper cases.

Sift the flour and salt into a large mixing bowl. Add the butter, caster sugar, soured cream, vanilla essence, zest, egg, egg yolks and milk. Beat with an electric beater set to medium speed for 2 minutes, or until combined and smooth.

Spoon the mixture evenly into the paper cases and bake for 15–20 minutes, or until golden and firm to the touch. A skewer inserted in the centre of a cupcake should come out clean. Cool on a wire rack.

To make the icing, mash the strawberries with a fork, combine with the icing sugar and beat until smooth. Add a little extra sifted icing sugar if needed. Spread over the cakes. Store in an airtight container once the icing has set.

Variations
To make lemon icing, combine 125g (4oz) of sifted icing sugar, 20g (¾oz) of softened butter and 1–2 tablespoons of lemon juice.

For orange cupcakes, substitute 125ml (4fl oz) of freshly squeezed orange juice for the milk and add 1 tablespoon of finely grated orange zest to the cake batter.

250g (8oz) fresh or frozen raspberries
250g (8oz) caster (superfine) sugar
300ml (½ pint) freshly squeezed lemon juice
chilled water, to dilute

Raspberry lemonade
Makes 750ml (1¼ pints)
Preparation time: 5 minutes

In the kitchen – Purée the raspberries, sugar and lemon juice in an electric blender until smooth. Strain the mixture and store it in a large bottle or easily transportable container. It will keep for up to 2 days in the refrigerator. Or you can make the lemonade ahead and freeze it in a plastic container until needed.

At the picnic – Pour the chilled raspberry lemonade into a large jug and dilute with chilled water to taste.

Posh
Picnic

375ml (12 fl oz) Pimms no. 1 cup
125ml (4 fl oz) gin
1 litre (1¾ pints) sparkling lemonade
125ml (4 fl oz) cranberry juice
ice cubes
strawberries, redcurrants or other fresh berries, to garnish
1 lemon, sliced, to garnish
mint leaves, to garnish

Pink Pimms
Serves 4–6
Preparation time: 5 minutes

In the kitchen – Chill the alcohol, lemonade and cranberry juice. Pack some ice cubes in a coolbag.
At the picnic – Fill one quarter of a large jug with ice cubes. Pour in the Pimms, gin, lemonade and cranberry juice. Stir well. Add strawberries, redcurrants and other berries, the lemon slices and the mint leaves. Serve immediately.

120ml (4fl oz) tequila
60ml (2fl oz) triple sec or Cointreau
60ml (2fl oz) freshly squeezed lime juice
ice cubes
slices of lime
salt

Margarita
Serves 2
Preparation time: 10 minutes

In the kitchen – Chill the alcohol. Pack some ice cubes in a coolbag and some salt in an airtight container.
At the picnic – Pour the tequila, triple sec and lime juice into a cocktail shaker. Add 6–8 ice cubes and shake well.

Rub the rims of two glasses with a slice of lime. Sprinkle a layer of salt onto a plate and dip the glasses into the salt. Strain the cocktail into the glasses and serve.

50g (2oz) butter
½ small brown onion, finely sliced
2 cloves garlic, crushed
1 large red mild chilli, seeds removed and chopped
625g (1¼lb) uncooked prawns, peeled and veins removed
2–3 tablespoons soured cream
juice of 1 lime
1 tablespoon chopped fresh flat-leaf parsley
1 tablespoon chopped fresh coriander (cilantro)
Tabasco sauce
salt and freshly ground black pepper

12 breadsticks or grissini
12 thin slices prosciutto or parma ham

Spiced prawn dip
Serves 6
Preparation time: 20 minutes

In the kitchen – Heat the butter in a large frying pan and cook the onion, garlic and chilli, stirring occasionally, for 7 minutes, or until the onions and chilli have softened. Add the prawns and cook for another 3–4 minutes stirring occasionally, until the prawns are done and have turned pink.

Transfer the mixture to a food processor and process using the pulse action until coarsely chopped. Add the soured cream and pulse again until combined. Don't over-process – the dip should not be smooth.

Transfer the dip to a bowl with a close-fitting lid and stir in the lime juice and herbs. Add a few drops of Tabasco sauce and season to taste with salt and freshly ground black pepper. Keep in the refrigerator until needed.
At the picnic – Serve the prawn dip with crackers, breadsticks or corn chips.

Prosciutto-wrapped breadsticks
Makes 12
Preparation time: 10 minutes

In the kitchen – Pack the breadsticks and prosciutto separately in airtight containers.
At the picnic – Separate the slices of prosciutto and wrap a slice around the middle of each breadstick, leaving a space at each end for a handle.

Filling:

4 chicken breasts, skin removed

375g (12oz) good quality pork sausages

175g (6oz) pancetta, cubed

grated zest of 1 lemon

1 teaspoon fresh thyme

1 tablespoon chopped fresh parsley

1 tablespoon chopped fresh sage

salt and freshly ground black pepper

1 egg, lightly beaten, to glaze

250ml (8fl oz) chicken stock

11g (½oz) sachet gelatine

Pastry:

175g (6oz) plain (all-purpose) flour

175ml (6fl oz) water

75g (3oz) lard, cubed

Raised chicken pie

Serves 6

Preparation time: 2 hours 40 minutes

In the kitchen – Cut the chicken into 1cm (½in) cubes. Remove the sausages from their casings and crumble the meat into a bowl. Add the chicken, pancetta, lemon zest and herbs and mix well. Season well with lots of salt and pepper.

Preheat the oven to 180°C (350°F), gas mark 4. Grease a raised pie mould or a 18cm (7in) deep round cake tin with a removable base.

To make the pastry, sift the flour and a pinch of salt into a bowl, and make a well in the centre. Bring the water and lard to the boil in a small saucepan. Pour the mixture into the centre of the flour and mix with a wooden spoon until combined. When the pastry is cool enough to handle, knead it to produce a smooth dough. The pastry must be used while still warm. Reserve a quarter of the pastry for the lid, keeping it warm. Roll out the rest until it is large enough to cover the base and sides of the pie mould and press firmly into place, smoothing any pleats and leaving a little over-hang. The pastry should be about 5mm (¼in) thick. Fill the pastry case with the filling.

Roll out the remaining pastry to form the lid. Press into place, dampen the edges with beaten egg and press together to seal. Trim the pastry and use any excess to make decorative shapes; brush the top of the pie with beaten egg. Cut a 1.5cm (¾in) diameter hole in the centre of the lid. Bake the pie for 2 hours, covering it with a double layer of greaseproof paper if the pastry starts to colour too quickly. Leave the pie to cool in the tin.

Heat the stock and stir in the gelatine until dissolved. Pour the mixture into the pie through the hole in the lid using a funnel. Leave for 24 hours before eating.

At the picnic – Transport the pie to the picnic in the pie mould or tin, then cut it into slices using a sharp knife.

3 chicken breasts
1 tablespoon olive oil
5 rashers bacon, chopped
4 thick slices white bread
2 tablespoons vegetable oil
1 large Cos lettuce
50g (2oz) freshly shaved Parmesan cheese
salt and freshly ground black pepper

Dressing:
4 anchovy fillets
1 clove garlic, crushed
2 tablespoons lemon juice
1 egg yolk
½ teaspoon Dijon mustard
4 tablespoons olive oil

Chicken Caesar salad
Serves 4–6
Preparation time: 45 minutes

In the kitchen – Preheat the oven to 200°C (400°F), gas mark 6. Brush the chicken breasts with olive oil and season. Roast for 15–20 minutes, or until cooked. Set aside to cool.

Fry the bacon over a medium heat for 5 minutes, or until crisp. Drain on kitchen paper.

Remove the crusts from the bread and cut the slices into 1.5 cm (¾in) cubes. Add the vegetable oil to the frying pan and fry the bread over a medium heat, tossing them constantly, until golden. Drain them on kitchen paper.

Place the dressing ingredients in a blender or food processor and pulse until combined. Season to taste and store in a screw-top jar in the refrigerator.

Separate the lettuce leaves, rinse and dry them with a clean tea towel. Pack the chicken, bacon, fried bread and lettuce in separate containers and store them in the refrigerator

At the picnic – Put the lettuce in a serving bowl. Slice the chicken and add it to the salad with the bacon and fried bread. Scatter over the Parmesan and drizzle with dressing.

The dressing contains a raw egg yolk: substitute 2 tablespoons of mayonnaise if you prefer.

Base:
200g (7oz) plain sweet biscuits
¼ teaspoon ground ginger
100g (3½ oz) unsalted butter, melted

Filling:
500g (1lb) cream cheese, softened
150g (5oz) caster (superfine) sugar
3 eggs, lightly beaten
125ml (4fl oz) double (heavy) cream
1 teaspoon vanilla essence
1 teaspoon finely grated lemon zest
2 teaspoons lemon juice

Cheesecake fingers
Makes 18 fingers
Preparation time: 45 minutes, plus chilling

In the kitchen – Grease a 20 x 30cm (8 x 12in) shallow cake tin and line the base and sides with baking paper, leaving extra paper hanging over the 2 long sides of the tin.

Place the biscuits and ginger in a food processor and pulse until crushed. Add the butter and process until the mixture comes together. Using your fingertips, press the crumb mixture into the base of the tin. Chill for 30 minutes.

Preheat the oven to 180°C (350°F), gas mark 4.

With an electric mixer, beat the cream cheese and caster sugar until creamy and well combined. Gradually add the eggs, beating well after each addition. Fold in the cream, vanilla, lemon zest and juice until smooth.

Spoon the mixture onto the prepared base and smooth the top. Bake for 25 minutes, or until pale golden and just set in the centre. Allow to cool, then chill for 6–12 hours. Transport the cheesecake to the picnic in the tin.

At the picnic – Use the overhanging paper to help remove the cheesecake. Cut it into fingers and serve.

There are no shortcuts to a posh picnic: everything has to be done properly – margaritas served in frosted glasses, a Caesar salad tossed at the picnic and served on china plates and a classic raised pie that has to be made a whole day in advance. Carry through the theme by using linen napkins, a crisp tablecloth and proper cutlery, though you may stop short of hiring a butler. With so much to carry this is one occasion where you won't want to walk far, so match the picnic to the event. A picnic with an impeccable pedigree is ideal for a day at the races, an open-air opera or theatre production. A folding table and chairs will preserve guests' finery from grass stains – and don't forget rugs in case the evening turns chilly.

Romantic Picnic

1 sheet ready-rolled puff pastry
2 tablespoons pesto
200g (7oz) cherry tomatoes
40g (1½oz) feta cheese or goat's cheese, crumbled
1 tablespoon chopped fresh basil or chives
salt and freshly ground black pepper

Tomato tartlets

Makes 2, as a starter
Preparation time: 30 minutes

In the kitchen – Preheat the oven to 200°C (400°F), gas
mark 6. Cut the pastry into two 12cm (5in) squares and
place them on a lightly greased baking sheet. Spread each
pastry square with pesto, leaving a 1.5cm (¾in) border.
Halve the tomatoes (or quarter them if large) and place them
on the pesto, being careful not to go over the border.

Place the tray in the top half of the oven and bake for
15 minutes. Remove the tray, sprinkle each tart with
crumbled cheese and season well with salt and freshly ground
black pepper. Return to the oven and continue to cook for
an extra 5 minutes, or until the pastry is golden and the
edges risen. Transfer the tarts onto a wire rack to cool.
Sprinkle with herbs.

Carefully wrap each tart in greaseproof paper and place in
a sealed plastic container to transport.

At the picnic – Serve the tarts topped with a little extra
crumbled cheese and herbs.

75g (3oz) cream cheese, softened at room temperature
2 teaspoons lemon juice
1 teaspoon chopped chives
4 slices white bread, crusts removed
150g (5oz) sliced smoked salmon
salt and freshly ground black pepper

Smoked salmon spirals

Serves 2, as a snack or starter
Preparation time: 10 minutes, plus chilling

In the kitchen – Using a large fork, beat the cream cheese,
lemon juice and chives together until soft and combined.
To make one roll-up, lay 2 slices of bread side by side on a
board, overlapping the edges by about 1cm (½inch). Use a
rolling pin and lightly roll the bread, sealing the edges
together as you do.

Spread with a thin layer of cream cheese and cover with
smoked salmon slices. Season with a little freshly ground
black pepper. Start from the short end and firmly roll up the
bread (like a Swiss roll) to form a log shape. Wrap tightly in
plastic wrap. Repeat with remaining slices of bread.
Refrigerate for up to 4 hours.

At the picnic – Transport the rolls to the picnic wrapped in
the plastic wrap. To serve, remove the plastic and slice each
roll into 4 rounds.

750g (1½lb) cooked medium prawns
1 tablespoon lemon juice
2 tablespoons olive oil
200g (7oz) can cannellini or white beans
1 tablespoon chopped chives
1 bunch asparagus, trimmed
50g (2oz) rocket (arugula) or baby salad leaves, to serve
2 small ripe avocados
salt and freshly ground black pepper

Sauce:
125ml (4fl oz) mayonnaise
1 tablespoon tomato ketchup
1 teaspoon lemon juice
Tabasco sauce

2 chicken breasts, skin removed
6 spring onions (scallions)
2cm (1¾ in) fresh ginger, finely sliced
1 lime, halved
1 tablespoon roughly chopped fresh coriander (cilantro)
1 tablespoon vegetable oil
1 tablespoon light soy sauce
1 teaspoon toasted sesame seeds
2 handfuls mixed salad leaves, to serve

Prawn and avocado salad
Serves 2, as a main course
Preparation time: 25 minutes

In the kitchen – Peel the prawns, place them in a bowl and pour over the lemon juice and olive oil. Drain and rinse the beans and add them to the prawns. Stir in the chives and season well with freshly ground black pepper. Store in an airtight container in the refrigerator.

To make the sauce, combine the mayonnaise, ketchup, lemon juice and a few drops of Tabasco. Taste and season then store the sauce in a screw-top jar in the refrigerator until needed for the picnic.

Cook the asparagus in a large pot of boiling salted water for 4 minutes, or until just tender. Drain, drizzle with a little extra oil and wrap in foil until ready to transport.

At the picnic – Divide the salad leaves between 2 plates. Peel, stone and halve the avocados and place 2 halves on each plate. Add some asparagus to each salad and top with the prawn and bean mixture. Drizzle with the sauce and season with salt and freshly ground black pepper.

Chinese-style chicken
Serves 2
Preparation time: 45 minutes, plus cooling

In the kitchen – Put the chicken, 3 spring onions, half the ginger and half a lime into a large saucepan. Add water to cover the chicken, place over a medium heat and bring to the boil. Simmer for 10 minutes, then remove from the heat, cover with a tight fitting lid and leave to cool.

Lift the chicken breasts from the saucepan, drain well and dry with kitchen paper.

Chop the flesh into bite-size pieces and place in an airtight container. Finely slice the remaining spring onions diagonally and finely chop the rest of the ginger. Stir the spring onions, ginger, coriander, oil, soy sauce and sesame seeds into the chicken mixture. Squeeze over the juice from the remaining lime half. Keep in the refrigerator until ready to transport to the picnic.

At the picnic – To serve, divide the mixture between 2 bowls and serve with the salad leaves.

100g (3½oz) blanched almonds
275g (9oz) plain (all-purpose) flour
1 teaspoon baking powder
250g (8oz) caster (superfine) sugar
2 teaspoons finely grated lemon zest
3 tablespoons chopped candied citrus peel
2 eggs, beaten
1 egg yolk

2 ripe peaches or nectarines
250g (8oz) raspberries
2 oranges

Lemon biscotti
Makes 25–30
Preparation time: 1 hour 45 minutes

In the kitchen –Preheat the oven to 180°C (350°F), gas mark 4.

Spread the almonds on a baking tray and bake them for 7–10 minutes, tossing occasionally, until they are lightly toasted. Leave them to cool then chop them roughly.

Sift the flour, baking powder and caster sugar into a mixing bowl. Stir in the zest, candied peel and almonds. Add the beaten eggs and extra yolk and mix to form a firm dough. If the dough is very sticky, add some extra flour.

Knead the dough on a floured surface for 5 minutes, or until smooth. Form into a flattened log about 30cm (12in) long. Place on a baking tray lined with baking paper. Bake for 35–40 minutes until golden. Cool on a wire rack.

Reduce the oven temperature to 120°C (250°F), gas mark ½. Line two baking trays with baking paper.

With a long serrated knife, carefully cut the log diagonally into 5mm (¼in) thick slices. The slices will be crumbly on the edges so work slowly and try to hold the slices as you cut. Arrange them in a single layer on the trays and return them to the oven for 25–35 minutes until dry and crisp, turning occasionally. Store in an airtight container for up to 2 weeks.

On-the-spot fruit salad
Serves 2
Preparation time: 5 minutes

In the kitchen – Wrap the peaches or nectarines carefully and pack them in a rigid container along with the raspberries and oranges.

At the picnic – Peel the peaches if desired, remove the stones and cut into slices. Place the slices in a bowl and scatter the berries over the peaches. Halve the oranges and squeeze the juice over the fruit.

200g (7oz) good quality dark chocolate
12–14 large strawberries

2 egg whites
pinch of salt
125g (4oz) caster (superfine) sugar
½ teaspoon white vinegar
½ teaspoon vanilla essence
1 teaspoon cornflour (corn starch)
crème fraîche
150g (5oz) fresh berries

Chocolate-dipped strawberries

Serves 2
Preparation time: 20 minutes

In the kitchen – Break the chocolate into small pieces and place in a small heat-proof bowl. Melt the chocolate by setting the bowl over a saucepan of hot (but not boiling) water, making sure the water doesn't touch the base of the bowl. Alternatively use a microwave to melt the chocolate. Stir occasionally until smooth.

Make sure the strawberries are completely dry. Even a single drop of water in the melted dark chocolate can cause the chocolate to 'seize' into a thick mess. Line a baking tray with non-stick baking paper.

Remove the saucepan from the heat, leaving the bowl of chocolate sitting over the hot water. Holding the stalk, dip each strawberry into the chocolate until nearly covered. Lay them on the lined tray to cool. Keep in a cool dry place until ready to transport to the picnic.

Meringues

Serves 6
Preparation time: 1 hour 10 minutes

In the kitchen – Preheat the oven to 120°C (250°F), gas mark ½. Draw four 9cm (3½in) diameter circles on a piece of baking paper, allowing space between each meringue for the mixture to spread. Use the paper to line a baking tray.

Place the egg whites and salt in a clean, dry bowl. Beat with electric beaters until soft peaks form. Gradually add the caster sugar, beating well after each addition. Beat until the mixture is stiff and glossy. Fold in the vinegar, vanilla and cornflour.

Using a large spoon, heap the mixture onto the circles on the baking paper. Shape into a circle with a spatula, leaving the centres slightly hollowed.

Bake the meringues for 50 minutes or until crisp on the outside. Turn off the oven and allow the meringues to cool in the oven with the door ajar. Carefully lift them off the baking paper and store in an airtight container until needed. They will keep for up to 2 weeks.

At the picnic – Top the meringues with some crème fraîche and berries.

50g (2oz) golden caster (superfine) sugar
½ teaspoon ground nutmeg
pinch chilli powder
2 tablespoons vegetable oil
250g mixed unsalted nuts: try macadamias, pecans,
    cashews, almonds and Brazil nuts – make a mixture
    of your personal favourites
salt and freshly ground black pepper

chilled champagne or sparkling wine
crème de cassis

Caramelized nuts

Serves 2
Preparation time: 10 minutes

In the kitchen – Put 1 tablespoon of sugar, the nutmeg and
chilli powder into a small dish. Heat the oil in a large
saucepan over a medium heat; add the nuts and remaining
sugar. Cook, stirring regularly for 5–7 minutes, or until the
sugar has melted and the nuts are slightly golden.

Tip the nuts into a large bowl and sprinkle over the sugar
and spice mixture. Toss well and season with salt and freshly
ground black pepper. Set aside to cool.

Once cool, store the nuts in an airtight container. They
will keep for up to 5 days.

Kir royale

Serves 2
Preparation time: 5 minutes, plus chilling

In the kitchen – There's no need to make kir royale with
vintage champagne, but a hint of cassis gives a young
sparkling wine a pretty rose colour and rounds off its flavour.
Choose a brut or a variety with as little sugar as possible.
Chill the wine and take to the picnic in a coolbag.
At the picnic – Place 1 teaspoon of crème de cassis at the
bottom of a fluted champagne glass and top off with bubbly.
Taste and add a little extra cassis if necessary.

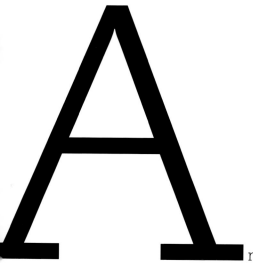n indulgent picnic for two should be a sensuous experience – tarts made with the lightest puff pastry or filo, chicken spiked with fresh ginger and herbs, followed by melt-in-the-mouth biscotti and meringues and voluptuous finger foods such as strawberries dipped in chocolate.

You'll notice that not one of these recipes contains a hint of garlic to spoil any post-picnic kisses. For the same reason choose your picnic spot carefully – you don't want to be disturbed by boisterous hikers, plagued by midges or contemplated by a herd of mournful cows. To drink, champagne or sparkling wine is the ultimate extravagance, turned a romantic shade of pink with a dash of crème de cassis. Take an armful of cushions, a rug or two and a big parasol, and enjoy an idyllic afternoon.

Winter
Picnic

2 tablespoons olive oil
1 onion, chopped
1 carrot, chopped
1 stick celery, chopped
2 cloves garlic, chopped
750g (1½lb) ripe tomatoes, quartered
1x 400g (13oz) can chopped tomatoes
1 litre (1¾pints) chicken stock or vegetable stock
250ml (8fl oz) water
salt and freshly ground black pepper

Tomato soup

Serves 4
Preparation time: 50 minutes

In the kitchen – Heat the olive oil in a large saucepan. Sauté the onion, carrot, celery and garlic for 5 minutes. Add the fresh tomatoes and cook for another 3–4 minutes.

Add the canned tomatoes, stock and water. Bring to the boil, reduce the heat and simmer for 30 minutes.

Remove from the heat and allow the soup to cool a little. Purée the soup in batches in a food processor or using a hand-held blender. Season to taste with salt and freshly ground black pepper.

Gently reheat the soup before transferring it to a warmed 2 litre (3½ pint) Thermos flask to transport it to the picnic.

At the picnic – Pour the soup into mugs and serve with Parmesan and Chilli Toasts (see page 88).

2 tablespoons vegetable oil
4 bacon rashers, chopped
2 leeks, chopped
1 onion, chopped
1 carrot, chopped
1 clove garlic, chopped
600g (1¼lb) sweet potato, peeled
    and cut into chunks
1.2 litres (2 pints) chicken or vegetable stock
salt and freshly ground black pepper
yogurt or soured cream (optional)
1 teaspoon chopped chives (optional)

Leek and sweet potato soup

Seves 4
Preparation time: 50 minutes

In the kitchen – Heat the oil in a large saucepan over a medium heat. Add the bacon and cook, stirring occasionally, for 2–3 minutes. Add the leeks, onion, carrot, garlic and sweet potato. Cook, stirring, for 5 minutes or until the leek and onion have softened.

Add the stock and bring to the boil. Cover and simmer for 25–30 minutes, until the vegetables are tender. Allow to cool a little, then purée the soup in batches in a food processor or using a hand-held blender.

Gently reheat the soup. You can thin it with a little water if it is too thick. Season to taste with salt and freshly ground black pepper.

Transfer the hot soup to a warmed 2 litre (3½ pint) Thermos flask to transport it to the picnic.

At the picnic – Pour the soup into mugs to serve. If you want to, add a dollop of yogurt or soured cream and some chopped chives.

1 French stick
1 tablespoon olive oil
handful of grated Parmesan cheese
½ teaspoon chopped fresh chilli
    or dried chilli flakes

2 tablespoons vegetable oil
6 slices smoked bacon, roughly chopped
1 brown onion, finely chopped
1 clove of garlic, crushed
2 tablespoons maple syrup
1 tablespoon treacle
2 teaspoons Dijon mustard
pinch chilli powder
1 x 400g (13oz) can cannellini beans
    or other beans, drained and rinsed
1 bay leaf
100ml (3½fl oz) water

Parmesan and chilli toasts

Serves 4
Preparation time: 15 minutes

In the kitchen – Preheat the oven to 180°C (350°F), gas
mark 4. Slice 8 diagonal slices, each about ½ cm (¼ in) thick,
from the bread and place them in a single layer on a baking
sheet. Brush lightly on both sides with olive oil and bake for
5–10 minutes, or until crisp. Turn them over halfway
through cooking. Remove the tray of toasts from the oven.

  Combine the grated Parmesan cheese with the chilli and
sprinkle over the toasts. Return them to the top shelf of the
oven and bake until hot. Set aside until cool, then transfer to
an airtight container ready to take to the picnic.

At the picnic – Serve the toasts with mugs of Tomato Soup
(see page 86)

Boston-style baked beans

Serves 4
Preparation time: 1 hour

In the kitchen – Heat the oil in a large frying pan and cook
the bacon for 2 minutes. Add the onion and garlic and cook,
stirring occasionally for 5 minutes or until the onion is soft,
but not browned. Add the maple syrup, treacle, mustard,
chilli powder, beans, bay leaf and water. Simmer over a
low heat for 45 minutes, stirring occasionally. The mixture
should be thick but add a little extra water if necessary
during cooking.

  Remove the bay leaf and transfer the hot beans to a
warmed wide-necked Thermos flask.

Picnics need not be limited to sunny summer days. Picnics on the beach out of season often mean you've got the shoreline to yourself and lots more space for games and fun than on a crowded summer day. There's nothing more bracing than a long winter walk fuelled by the knowledge that there's a flask of hot soup in your backpack. The key is to match the food to the weather – that means robust soups, substantial bean dishes like Boston-style baked beans that can be kept warm in a wide-necked food flask, and chicken drumsticks with a hint of warming chilli. A flask of mocha coffee is all the more welcome fortified with a nip of something stronger. If you take a rug to sit on, choose one with a waterproof backing for obvious reasons or travel light and perch on a stile or fallen tree trunk to savour your winter picnic.

1 tablespoon cornflour (corn starch)
250g (8oz) natural yogurt
2 tablespoons fresh harissa (North African chilli paste)
4 tablespoons chopped fresh flat-leaf parsley
4 tablespoons chopped fresh coriander (cilantro) leaves
½ teaspoon salt
juice of 1 lemon, plus 1 lemon
8 chicken drumsticks

ground coffee beans or instant coffee granules
150g (5oz) good quality dark chocolate,
    broken into pieces
1 tablespoon granulated sugar
500ml (17fl oz) milk
dash of brandy, whisky or a flavoured liqueur
    such as Frangelico or Grand Marnier (optional)

Spiced chicken drumsticks
Serves 4–6
Preparation time: 40 minutes plus marinating

In the kitchen – Combine the cornflour, yogurt, harissa, herbs, salt and lemon juice. With a sharp knife make a couple of slits on each drumstick. Place the chicken in a ceramic or glass dish, spread with the yogurt mixture and set aside to marinate for 30 minutes.

Preheat the oven to 200°C (400°F), gas mark 6.

Place the drumsticks on a rack in a baking tray and cook, turning occasionally, for 30–35 minutes, or until golden and cooked through. Allow them to cool before packing in a container to take to the picnic.

At the picnic – Serve the drumsticks with the lemon cut into wedges – best eaten with your fingers.

Mocha
Serves 4–6
Preparation time: 15 minutes

In the kitchen – Make a cafetière or pot of freshly brewed coffee, or a jug of instant coffee.

Put the chocolate, sugar and milk in a small saucepan. Place over a low heat and stir until the sugar and chocolate have melted and the mixture is smooth. As it comes to the boil, whisk to create a bit of froth and remove from the heat.

Pour the hot chocolate mixture into a warmed 1 litre (1¾ pint) Thermos flask and top up with the hot coffee. Taste and add extra sugar if necessary. Add the brandy or liqueur if you like.

125g (4oz) unsalted butter, softened
150g (5oz) soft light brown sugar
125g (4oz) crunchy peanut butter
1 egg
175g (6oz) self-raising (self-rising) flour, sifted
100g (3½oz) dark chocolate chips

125g (4oz) good-quality dark chocolate, chopped
125g (4oz) unsalted butter, chopped
1 egg
200g (7oz) soft light brown sugar
150g (5oz) self-raising (self-rising) flour, sifted
50g (2oz) dark chocolate chips

Peanut butter cookies
Makes 24–30
Preparation time: 25 minutes plus chilling

In the kitchen – Preheat the oven to 180°C (350°F), gas mark 4. Line two oven trays with baking paper.

In a mixing bowl, beat the butter and brown sugar with an electric beater for 3 minutes, or until fluffy and well combined. Add the peanut butter and beat well. Break the egg into the bowl and beat until combined. Stir in the flour until well mixed. Chill the mixture for 20 minutes.

Drop tablespoons of the dough from a spoon onto the oven trays, leaving a 5cm (2in) space between each to allow the biscuits to spread while cooking.

Bake for 12–15 minutes, or until the biscuits are firm to the touch. Allow them to sit on the tray for 5 minutes to firm before transferring to a wire rack to cool. Store in an airtight container.

At the picnic – Serve the cookies with a cup of coffee or Mocha (see page 91).

Fudgy chocolate cookies
Makes 24–30
Preparation time: 25 minutes plus chilling

In the kitchen – Preheat the oven to 180°C (350°F), gas mark 4). Line two oven trays with baking paper.

Melt the chocolate and butter in a small bowl set over a saucepan of gently simmering water, making sure the water doesn't touch the base of the bowl. Stir occasionally, until smooth. Alternatively use a microwave to melt the chocolate.

In a separate bowl, beat the egg and brown sugar with a wooden spoon until combined.

Stir the chocolate mixture into the egg mixture. Add the flour and mix until smooth and thick. Chill the dough for 20 minutes.

Drop teaspoonfuls of the dough onto the oven trays, leaving 5cm (2in) space between each to allow the biscuits to spread while cooking.

Cook for 7–10 minutes, or until the biscuits are firm to the touch and the tops have wrinkled slightly. Transfer to a wire rack to cool, then store in an airtight container.

At the picnic – Serve the cookies with coffee or Mocha (see page 91).

Index

To FM with love

First published in 2004 by Conran Octopus Limited,
a part of Octopus Publishing Group,
2–4 Heron Quays, London E14 4JP
www.conran-octopus.co.uk
Reprinted in 2004, 2005

Publishing Director: Lorraine Dickey
Senior Editor: Katey Day
Art Director: Chi Lam
Design: Carl Hodson
Photography: David Loftus
Stylist: Harriet Docker
Production Manager: Angela Couchman
Home Economy: David Herbert

British Cataloguing-in-Publication Data.
A catalogue record for this book is available from the British Library

ISBN 1 84091 358 4

To order please ring Conran Octopus Direct
on 01903 828503

Printed and bound in China